D1098576

TALKING TURKEYS

Bromley Libraries
30128 80188 003 3

BENJAMIN **ZEPHANIAH**

TALKING TURKEYS

PUFFIN BOOKS

PUFFIN BOOKS

Published by the Penguin Group
Penguin Books Ltd, 80 Strand, London WC2R 0RL, England
Penguin Putnam Inc., 375 Hudson Street, New York, New York 10014, USA
Penguin Books Australia Ltd, 250 Camberwell Road, Camberwell, Victoria 3124, Australia
Penguin Books Canada Ltd, 10 Alcorn Avenue, Toronto, Ontario, Canada M4V 3B2
Penguin Books India (P) Ltd, 11 Community Centre, Panchsheel Park, New Delhi – 110 017, India
Penguin Books (NZ) Ltd, Cnr Rosedale and Airborne Roads, Albany, Auckland, New Zealand
Penguin Books (South Africa) (Pty) Ltd, 24 Sturdee Avenue, Rosebank 2196, South Africa

Penguin Books Ltd, Registered Offices: 80 Strand, London WC2R 0RL, England

www.penguin.com

First published by Viking 1994
Published in Puffin Books 1995
032

Text copyright © Benjamin Zephaniah, 1994
Illustrations copyright © The Point, 1994
All rights reserved

The moral right of the author has been asserted

Filmset in Sabon and Frutiger

Made and printed in Great Britain by Clays Ltd, St Ives plc

Except in the United States of America, this book is sold subject to the condition that it shall not, by way of trade or otherwise, be lent, re-sold, hired out, or otherwise circulated without the publisher's prior consent in any form of binding or cover other than that in which it is published and without a similar condition including this condition being imposed on the subsequent purchaser

www.greenpenguin.co.uk

Penguin Books is committed to a sustainable future for our business, our readers and our planet. This book is made from Forest Stewardship Council™ certified paper.

Dedicated to the Earth

and the children who care

CONTENTS

TURKEY TALK 10
Greet tings 12
Body Talk 14
Running 16
Fear Not 18
Little Sister 20
Friends 22
According to My Mood 24
Royal Tea 26
How's Dat 28
Vegan Delight 30
Open Market 32
Multi-Culture 32
Food for Thought 33
Mr Candyman 34
A Day in the Life of Danny the Cat 36
Drivosaurus Rex 40
Part Wan 42
Part Two 42
Wordology 43
De Generation Rap 44
Solidarity 46
Medieval Religious Tribal Chant 47
Who's Who 48
Rap Connected 50
A Killer Lies 52
Heroes 54
Beyond de Bell 56

Civil Lies 58
POEMS FROM THE LAST PERSON ON EARTH 60
For Sale 62
A Beetle called Derek 64
Beat It 66
Pets Control 67
Memories 68
Think Me 70
MORE TURKEY TALK 72
I 74
Letters 74
Kiss an Tell 75
Over de Moon 76
Movie Madness 78
Fair Play 80
Jude 81
Telling Off 82
Luv Song 83
Eye See 84
Remembrance Days 86
Everyday 87
Talking Turkeys!! 88
Christmas Wise 90
Sunnyside Up 92
Once Upon a Time 93

TURKEY TALK

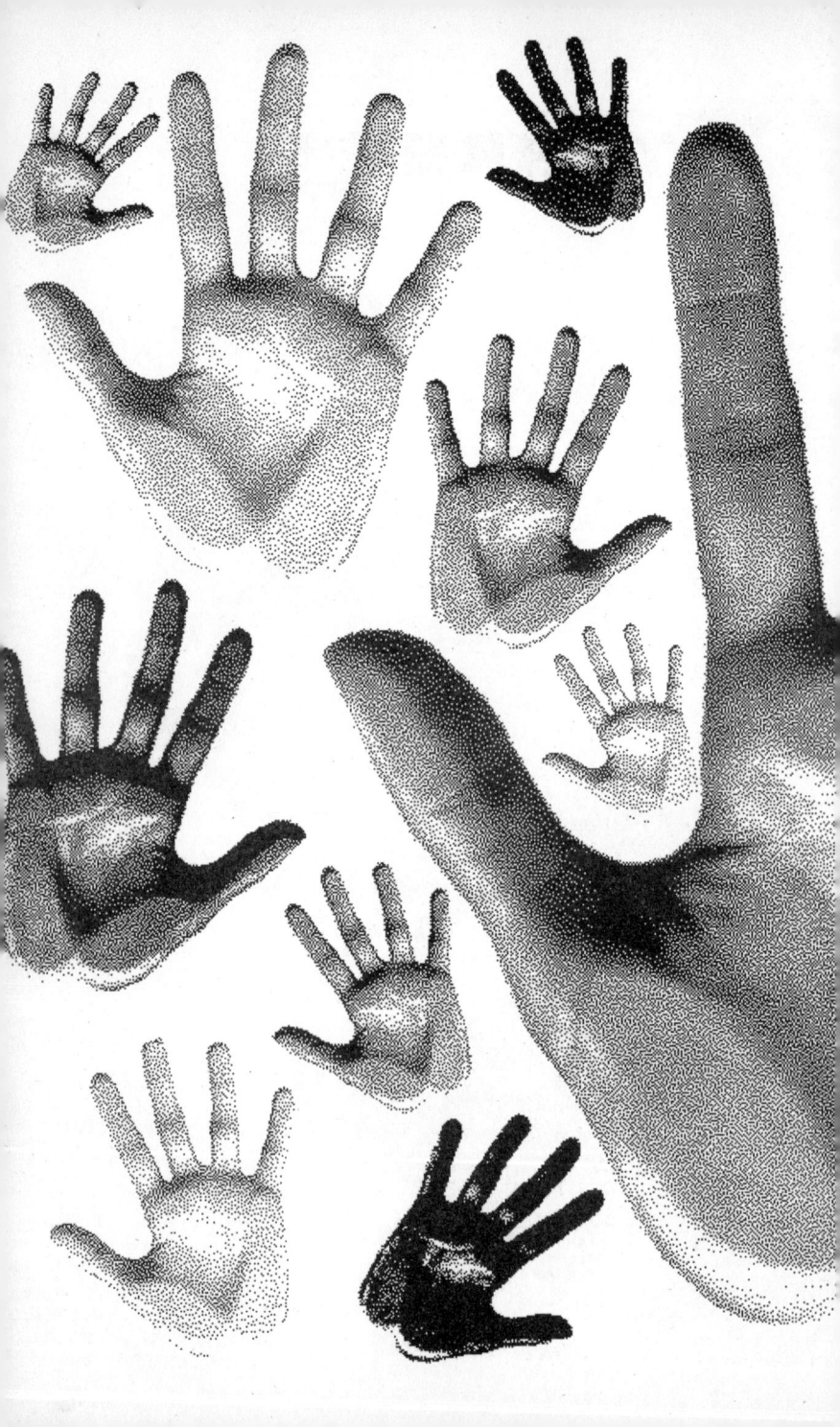

GREET TINGS

Assalaam Alaikum
Hola
Szia
Sat Srii Akaal
Wa Happen
Zdravo
Yia Sou
Merhaba
Hej
Yo
Sawast Dee Craap
Ciao
Zdravstvuyte
Endemenesh
Ahoj
Bonjour
Yassou
Shalom
Namaste
Dag
Guten Tag
Buenos Dias
Parev
Ehida
Selamat Datong
Dia Dhuit
Hallo
And Welcome

BODY TALK

Dere's a Sonnet
Under me bonnet
Dere's a Epic
In me ear,
Dere's a Novel
In me navel
Dere's a Classic
Here somewhere.
Dere's a Movie
In me left knee
A long story
In me right,
Dere's a shorty
Inbetweeny
It is tickly
In de night.
Dere's a picture
In me ticker
Unmixed riddims
In me heart,
In me texture
Dere's a comma
In me fat chin
Dere is Art.

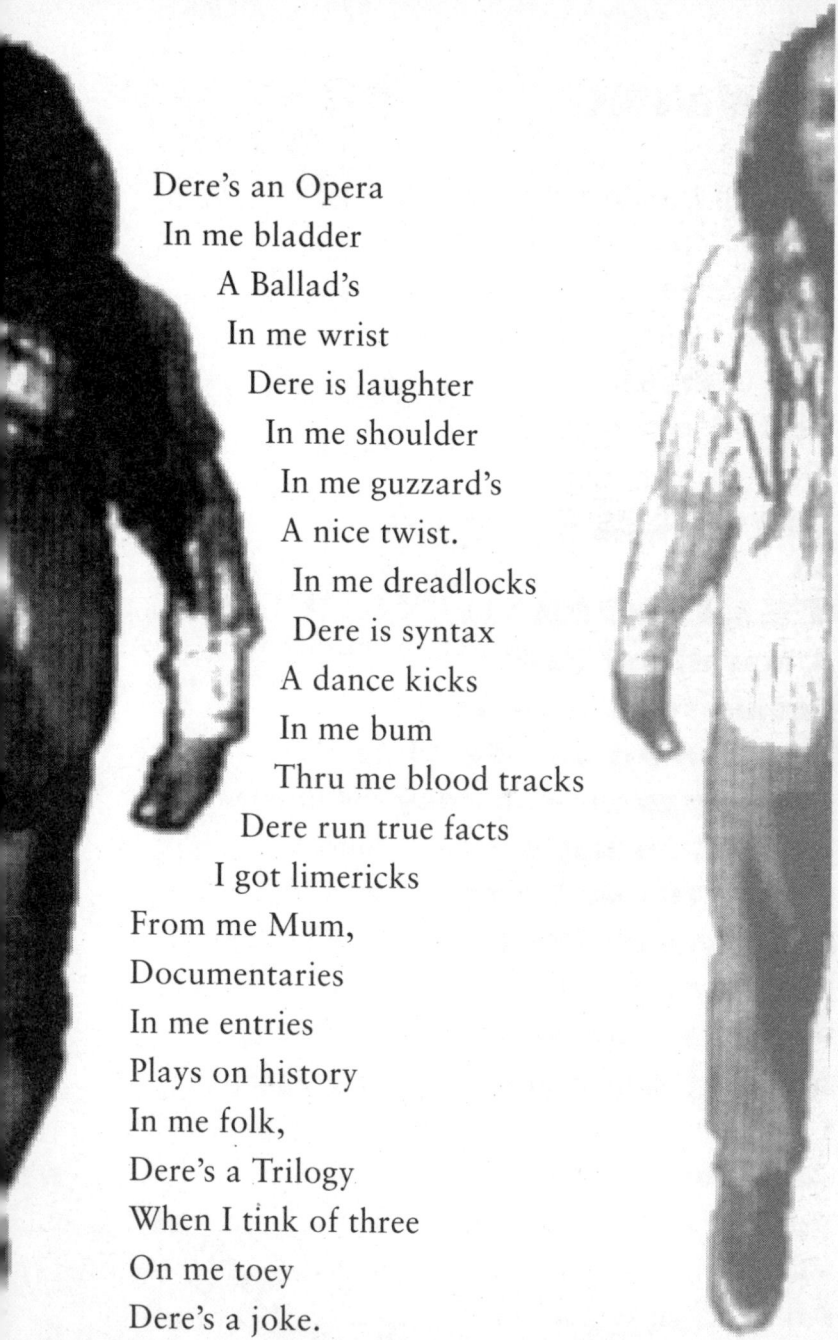

Dere's an Opera
In me bladder
A Ballad's
In me wrist
Dere is laughter
In me shoulder
In me guzzard's
A nice twist.
In me dreadlocks
Dere is syntax
A dance kicks
In me bum
Thru me blood tracks
Dere run true facts
I got limericks
From me Mum,
Documentaries
In me entries
Plays on history
In me folk,
Dere's a Trilogy
When I tink of three
On me toey
Dere's a joke.

RUNNING

I reckon I could run de world,
I used to run me school,
Hundred metres an two hundred metres,
I could run up Mount Everest
Wid a drink,
I could run tings wid big words
Like,
INFRASTRUCTURE,
an
TELECOMMUNICATION,
A marathon? Easy.
I could run out of bounds,
I run wild all de time
I run tings nice...as dey sey in Jamaica,
Or cool...as dey sey in Iceland,
I could run de Universe...in verse
But I haven't been given a chance.
I will get my chance,
Politicians are running outta ideas,
Dat may mean dat we all, you and me,
I an I,
All of we, may hav to run our own lives,
Dats bad...as dey sey in New York,
Way out...as dey sey in space,
All right...as dey sey in

Llanfairpwllgwy

gyllgogerchwyrndrobwll-llantysiliogogogoch.

FEAR NOT

Wanna be in our gang?
We cause Peace,
Fighters fear us,
On de streets
We shout slogans
Like,
Peace an Luv
One race, de Human Race
Make Patties Not War
An
Kiss a lip.

We are very safe
Animal friendly
Flower power crazy
Whole wheat flour fans.
We are de listening gang,
We want yu to say yes,
More,
Do it,
Go save everything.

Our only enemy is Ignorance
When we see it we rap it
In questions,
Reasoning an openmindedness,
We recycle ideas
An produce true stories,
Your stories,
Her stories an his
stories,
Wid luv stories.

We hav no words for things like,
Join us,
We luv yu baby
We luv yu people
We luv yu grasshopper.

LITTLE SISTER

That's my little sister
Just five minutes old
Already seeking something
To bite and chew and hold,
That's my little sister
Already going bald
I can't just call her sister
So what will she be called?

I want to call her Carol
But all carols are hymns
I want to call her Jimmy
But I always visit gyms,
I want to call her spotty
But she may punch my nose
I will not call her Rosy
She don't look like a rose.

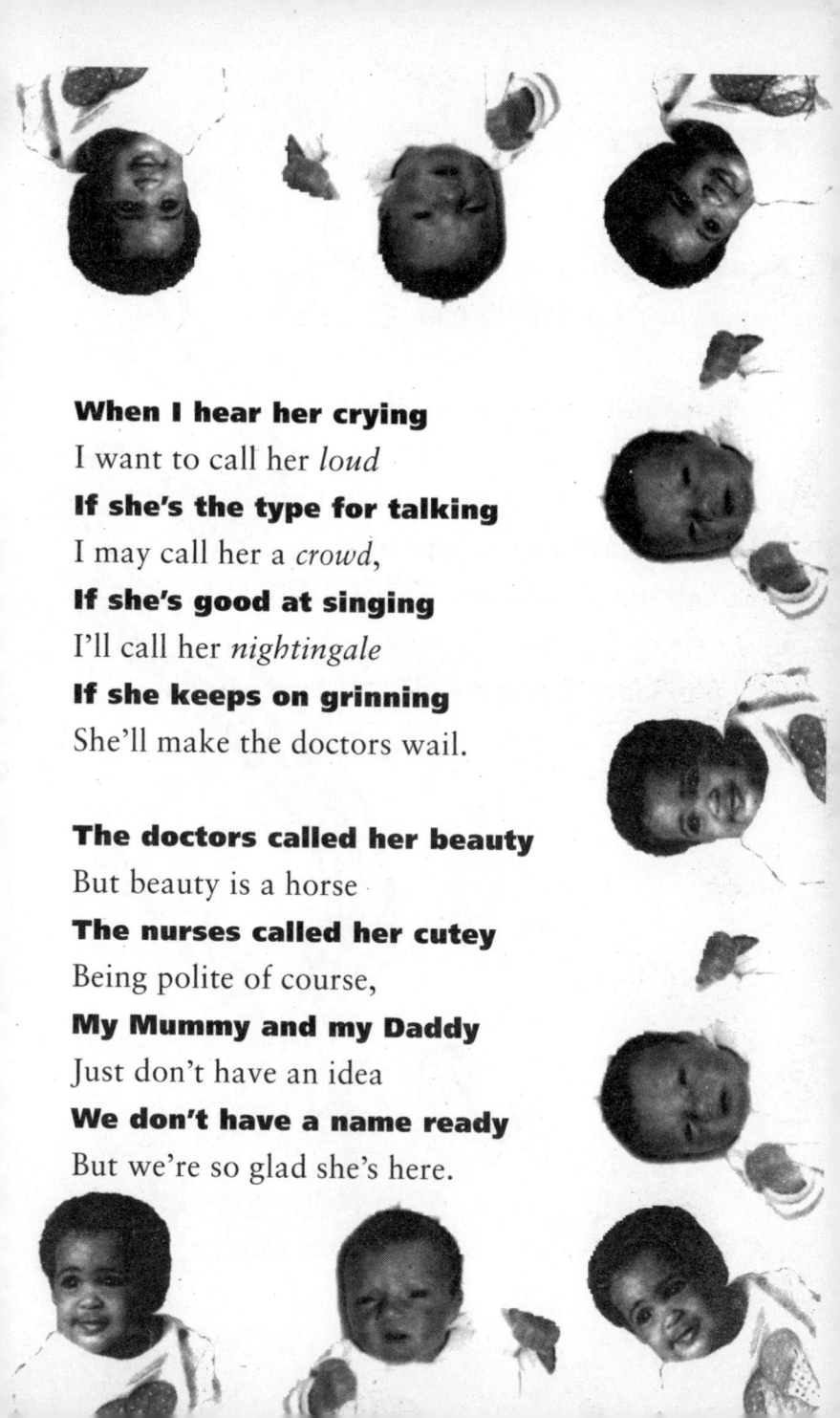

When I hear her crying
I want to call her *loud*
If she's the type for talking
I may call her a *crowd*,
If she's good at singing
I'll call her *nightingale*
If she keeps on grinning
She'll make the doctors wail.

The doctors called her beauty
But beauty is a horse
The nurses called her cutey
Being polite of course,
My Mummy and my Daddy
Just don't have an idea
We don't have a name ready
But we're so glad she's here.

FRIENDS

Funky monkey in the tree
I like when you talk to me
What I really like the best
Is when you bang upon my chest.

Slippery snake I am your mate
When all others hesitate
I'll be there right by your side
I am known to slip and slide.

♥ Hop along, croak croak, how ya doing **frog?**
No one understands our deep dialogue
People may laugh when they see us on the road
We must stick together
Monkey, snake, me, you and **toad**.

ACCORDING TO MY MOOD

I have *poetic* **licence**, i WriTe thE way i waNt.

i *drop* my **full** stops where *i* like...

MY CAPITAL LeteRs go where i liKE,

i **order** from **MY** PeN, i verse **the way** i like

(i do *my spelling write* **)**

Acording to My *MO*od.

i **HA**ve Poetic **licence**,

i put my **commers** where **i** like,,(((O).

(((my brackets *are* **write**((

I REPEAT **WH**en i likE.

i can't **go rong.**

i *look* and **i.e.**

It's rite.

i**I** REPEAT **WH**en i likE. **i have**

poetic **licence**!

don't question me**?**?? ?

J
J

ROYAL TEA

I went to Buckingham Palace today
To see where the Queen and her family stay
I went to Buckingham Palace today
To see the Queen's horses and men,
The Queen had gone shopping
A friend let us in
A very big chap with a very
big grin
He put all the money I had in a tin
Security checked me and then,
He showed me a picture three hundred years old
Kept in a frame made of valuable gold
I told him I had one just like it indoors
And that I may sell it to help a good cause,
A chandelier he said was priceless was nice
I said my one's better and it has a price
I went in a big room and saw a big throne
Just like the one my Mum has at home.

I saw carpets on walls that were not for sale
I met the man who sorts out royal mail
I went in the room where the Queen has her balls
And in there I saw some more carpets on walls,
On high polished floors I had a good slide
I got a good telling off from the guide

That very big chap with the very big grin
Now looked even
bigger was not smiling,
I said in his ear that I needed to
Pay a quick visit to the royal loo
It took fifteen minutes to get
myself there
Upon the loo door it said
'Kilroy waz ere'
Cameras filmed me on
return to reception
I signed autographs for my royal connections
I left a note for the Queen saying she can
Visit me anytime she's in East Ham.

I went to Buckingham Palace today
To see where the Queen and her family stay
I went to Buckingham Palace today
To see royal things old and new,
It cost me eight fifty but no need to worry
If you visit me you don't need any money
There's no OBEs
but there's fresh tea
with honey
And I can take
photos of **you**.

HOW'S DAT

No Sir
I don't play Cricket,
One time I try
Fearing a duck
I watch de ball fly towards me,
I recall every spin
An unforgettable air speed,
It bounced before me
Jus missing a two-day-old ant,
Up it cum
A red flash
Lick me finger so hard
I thought me finger would die.

Teacher tell me
I am good at cricket,
I tell teacher
I am not,
Teacher tell me
We love cricket,
I tell teacher
Not me,
I want Trigonometry
Fe help me people,
Teacher tell me
I am a born Cricketer,
But I never...well only once,
I don't play cricket.

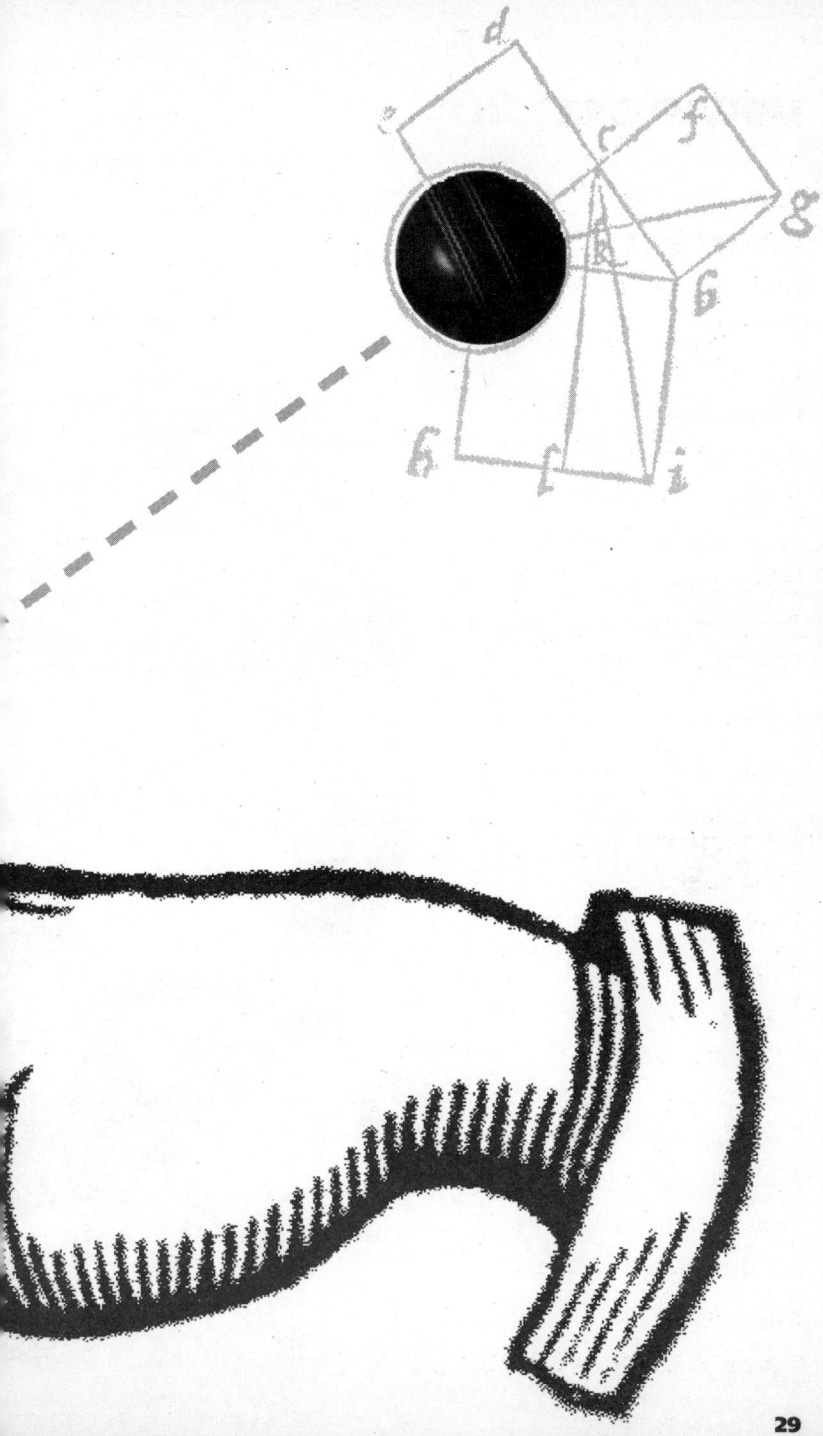
d
e
c
f
g
h
b
a
l
i

VEGAN DELIGHT

Ackees, chapatties
Dumplins an nan,
Channa an rotis
Onion uttapam,
Masala dosa
Green callaloo
Bhel an samosa
Corn an aloo.
Yam an cassava
Pepperpot stew,
Rotlo an guava
Rice an tofu,
Puri, paratha
Sesame casserole,
Brown eggless pasta
An brown bread rolls.

Soya milked muesli
Soya bean curd,
Soya sweet sweeties
Soya's de word,
Soya bean margarine
Soya bean sauce,
What can mek medicine?
Soya of course.

Soya meks yoghurt
Soya ice-cream,
Or soya sorbet
Soya reigns supreme,
Soya sticks liquoriced
Soya salads
Try any soya dish
Soya is bad.

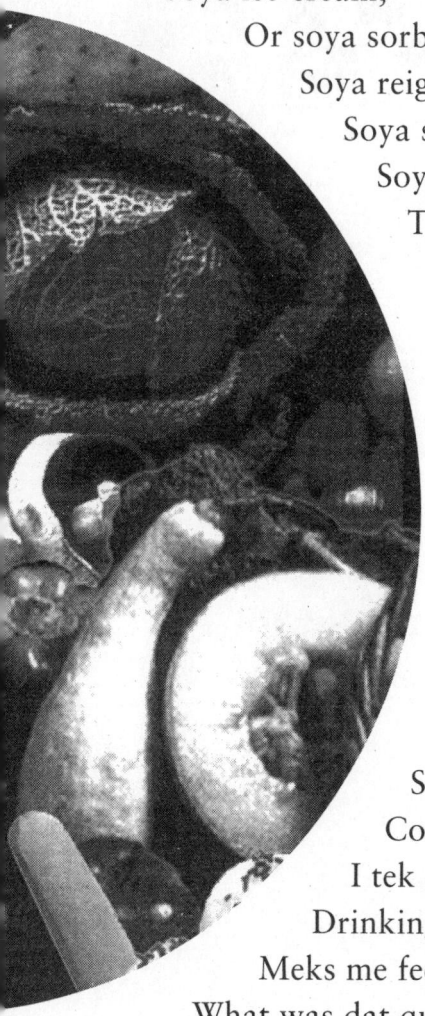

Plantain an tabouli
Cornmeal pudding
Onion bhajee
Wid plenty cumin,
Breadfruit an coconuts
Molasses tea
Dairy free omelettes
Very chilli.
Ginger bread, nut roast
Sorrell, paw paw,
Cocoa an rye toast
I tek dem on tour,
Drinking cool maubi
Meks me feel sweet,
What was dat question now?

What do we eat?

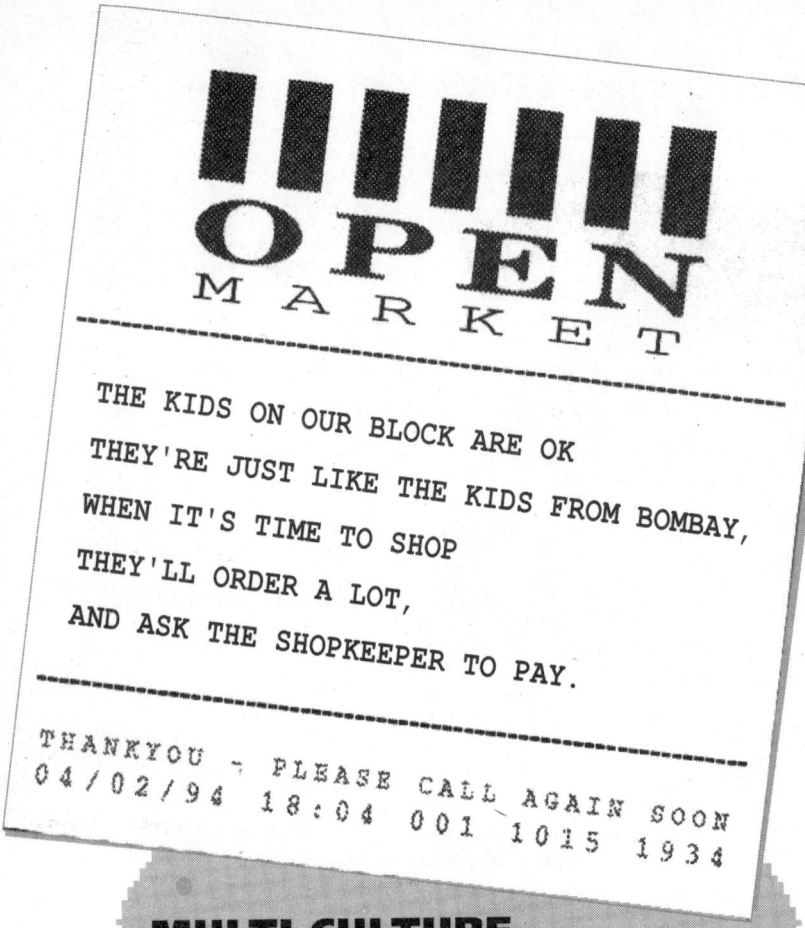

MULTI-CULTURE

I really luv chapatties
I eat dem all de time,
Today Iqbal made ten of dem
An nine of dem were mine,
I am krazy over mangoes
I once grew a mango tree,
My mango tree grew chapatties
Especially for me.

FOOD FOR THOUGHT

Fed up with your old dog food
Try new '**Johnny**'.
Johnny contains all the
goodness your dog needs.
Ideal for weight watching dogs,
Bite size pieces means less chewing for doggy
Lots of juicy gravy means doggy gets a stiff drink
And a happy dog means you're happy.
Look,
When confronted with 'some other dog food'
Your dog may wag its tail,
With new **Johnny** tails go krazy
Ears flip flop
Everything goes shaky, shaky, shaky,
Guard dogs don't fear
Johnny is here,
At prices some people can afford.

We spoke to Mrs Pal, a top breeder,
She said
'Get lost',
Then we spoke to Mr P.Chum,
He said
'I like it, I like it'.
Try new **Johnny** from Bite and
Barkers,
Dogs would chose **Johnny**,
Johnny tastes so good.

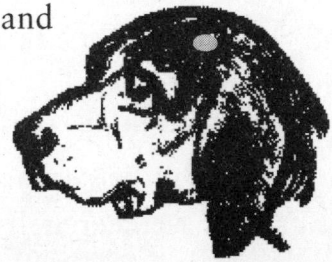

Bite and Barkers products
are not tested on animals.

MR CANDYMAN

★ **Candyman, Candyman**

Give me a sweet
Sugar free
And carob coated
I deserve a treat
I've been working so hard
Counting all me toes
Looking at me garden
Watching how it grows.
Dear Mr Candyman
I don't have ten pence
But I may just sell dis poem
If it can make sense,
If I even sell one line
You can eat with me
Or we can buy a seed
And plant an apple tree.

★ **Thanks Mr Candyman**

It's a lovely colour
I think I may cut it in half
And share it with me brother,
If me brother likes it
He may just buy me poem
We're poor but we do part exchange
That's how we keep going.

LOVE
GOOD PALS
HEART THROB
FUN TIME
LUCKY BOY

A DAY IN THE LIFE OF DANNY THE CAT

Danny wakes up
Eats
Finds a private place in the garden,
He returns
Plays with the plants
And sleeps.
Danny wakes up
Eats
Inspects the garden
Finds a cosy place
And sleeps.
Danny wakes up
Comes indoors
Inspects the carpet
Scratches himself
And sleeps.
Danny wakes up
Goes in the garden
Over the fence
Has a fight with Ginger
Makes a date with Sandy
Climbs on to next door's shed
And sleeps.

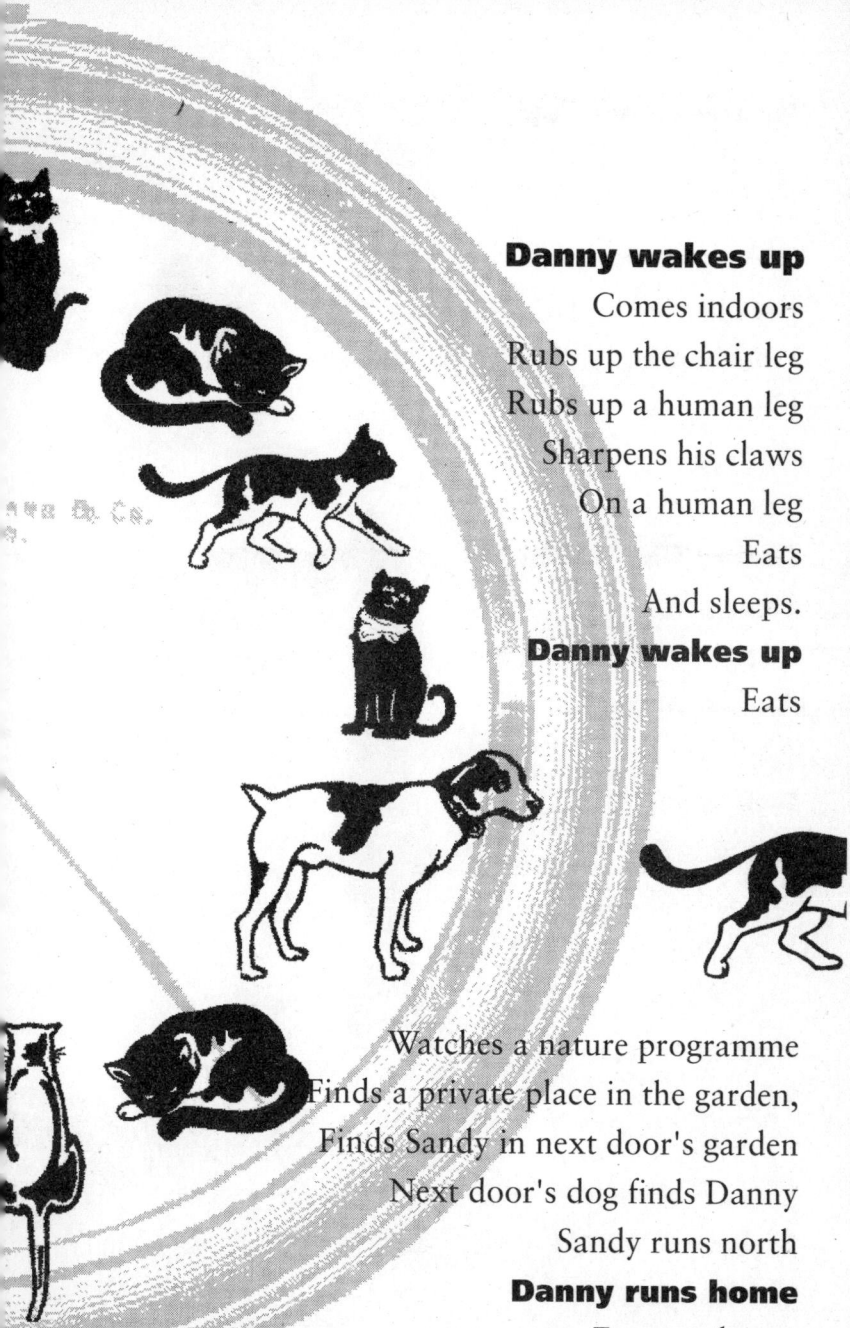

Danny wakes up
Comes indoors
Rubs up the chair leg
Rubs up a human leg
Sharpens his claws
On a human leg
Eats
And sleeps.
Danny wakes up
Eats

Watches a nature programme
Finds a private place in the garden,
Finds Sandy in next door's garden
Next door's dog finds Danny
Sandy runs north
Danny runs home
Eats an sleeps.

Danny wakes up
Checks for mice
Checks for birds
Checks for dogs
Checks for food
Finds a private place in the garden
Eats
And sleeps.

Danny has hobbies,
Being stroked
Car watching
And smelling feet

He loves life,
Keeps fit
And keeps clean,
Every night he covers himself
In spit,
Then he eats
And sleeps.

Benji
Danny

DRIVOSAURUS REX

The dinosaurs are back
Working at Hollywood
Now they are not flesh and bone
They're plastic, foam and wood
The dinosaurs are here
I saw one on a bus
As I was on the way to play
At Dinosaurs 'R' Us.

They came from Noah's Ark
Unto Jurassic Park
When they ete you can bet
They did some great big
Barks,
Then from Jurassic Park
Some came into our homes
In big boxes of cereals
With added rocks and stones.

The dinosaurs are back
With bottom, front and side
The ones I've seen look kind
of mean
And really very wide,
These dinosaurs are stars
I've seen them on radars
Looking cool and deadly
As they drive around in cars.

PART WAN

I wonder how babies are made,

All babies

Homosapien babies,

Donkey babies,

Bird babies.

Animals kiss

An den what

Babies.

Dere mus be more to it.

PART TWO

Life has its ups an downs
Even captives smile
I wonder why people die?
Dere mus be more to it.

WORDOLOGY

Sociologists

Physicists

Archaeologists

And

Anthropologists

Like

Dieticians

Rhetoricians

Mathematicians

And

Politicians

Are simple people,

Help them.

DE GENERATION RAP

Dat guy **BAD**
He's ***kicking***,
He's *wicked*,
CRUCIAL,
Cums round *here*
Wida **smiley** pon his face,
He CHILLS out,
Slides round,
Mekin circles,
He's **safe**.

Dis sista hard
She's *irie*,
MENTAL
RESPECT due,
She steps *cool*
Trods *easy*,
Hangs **tuff**,
Big up
An *vitalistic*.

When him pass thru
HARD VIBES,
Him *wild*,
Is a neat dude
SLICK geeza
A *natural* bro.
Made up.
She jus **OOW**,
Streetwise G,
She's **covered**
Fit, *Irie*,
X.

People on de **streets**
Luv dem so much,
Dem **jus call** dem
Drr Read full.

SOLIDARITY

An army of militant greens
In bio-degradable genes
Shout **'Give peas a chance**
An lettuce all dance
In unity wid butter beans'.

MEDIEVAL RELIGIOUS TRIBAL CHANT

(Please repeat)

WHO'S WHO

I used to think **nurses**
Were women,
I used to think **police**
Were men,
I used to think **poets**
Were boring,
Until **I** became one of **them.**

Poet

RAP CONNECTED

We were born to rap
We were born to dance
We were born to sing
We are Queens an Kings
We were born to live de life dat we luv
We were born to luv de life dat we live,
We were born to twist

We were born to shout
We can keep it in
We can hang it out
We got riddim in us mate

Get infected,
Shout it loud,
We are connected.

We were born to share
An hav fun whilst here,
So if you don't care
Go somewhere you square,
If you are aware
You will be respected
We all share the air and
We are connected.
We are black an brown
We are white an sound
We have pride of place
We are on de case
We are wild an tame
We are all de same
Sister, brother, kid,
We are connected.

A KILLER LIES

He's a Fox Hunter, he said
'Foxes need controlling, they spread germs
They're always mating.'
I think he's exaggerating,
He's a Fox Hunter, he said
'They're wild animals, they eat lambs and they eat chickens.'
He needs chickens for his kitchen.

He calls foxes beast,
But he collects their teeth,
He kills thousands every year
Once he whispered in me ear,
'It will kill you with its bite
That is why fox hunting's right,
Can't you sense they are evil
So unlike hunting people,
They are the enemy of our community
I love it when they're caught
And they make such good sport,
I never tasted one
When our hounds get them they're gone,
I am good at this you know
I'm a kind of Hunt hero.'

He's a Fox Hunter
His Daddy taught him well
When his hounds scent de smell
Excitement meks him yell,
He's a Fox Hunter
Know him by his killer eyes
Something dead must be his prize
He's de kind dat's **civilized.**

HEROES

Heroes are funny people, dey are lost an found
Sum heroes are brainy an sum are muscle-bound,

Plenty heroes die poor an are heroes
after dying
Sum heroes mek yu smile when yu
feel like crying.
Sum heroes are made heroes as a political trick
Sum heroes are sensible an sum are very thick!
Sum heroes are not heroes cause dey do not play de
game
A hero can be young or old and have a silly name.
Drunks an sober types alike hav heroes of dere kind
Most heroes are heroes out of sight an out of mind,
Sum heroes shine a light upon a place where
darkness fell
Yu could be a hero soon, yes, yu can never tell.
So if yu see a hero, better treat dem wid respect
Poets an painters say heroes are a prime subject,
Most people hav heroes even though some don't
admit
I say we're all heroes if we do our little bit.

BEYOND DE BELL

Yu push
Yu shove
Believing
School moves round **yu**,
Yu spy an lie
Believing
Tings control by **yu**,
What mek **yu** tink like dat?
Never mind
Academic ability
Concentration span
I.Q. business
Yu big in de playground,
Never mind
People who
Don't push an shove,
Yu do.

Table may turn
Yu may be pushed,
An macho boy
Yu may lose **yu** watch
Yu ill gained sweet money
Yu bigheadedness,
Table may turn
Yu may be shoved
Den walked over
By an army
Of carers

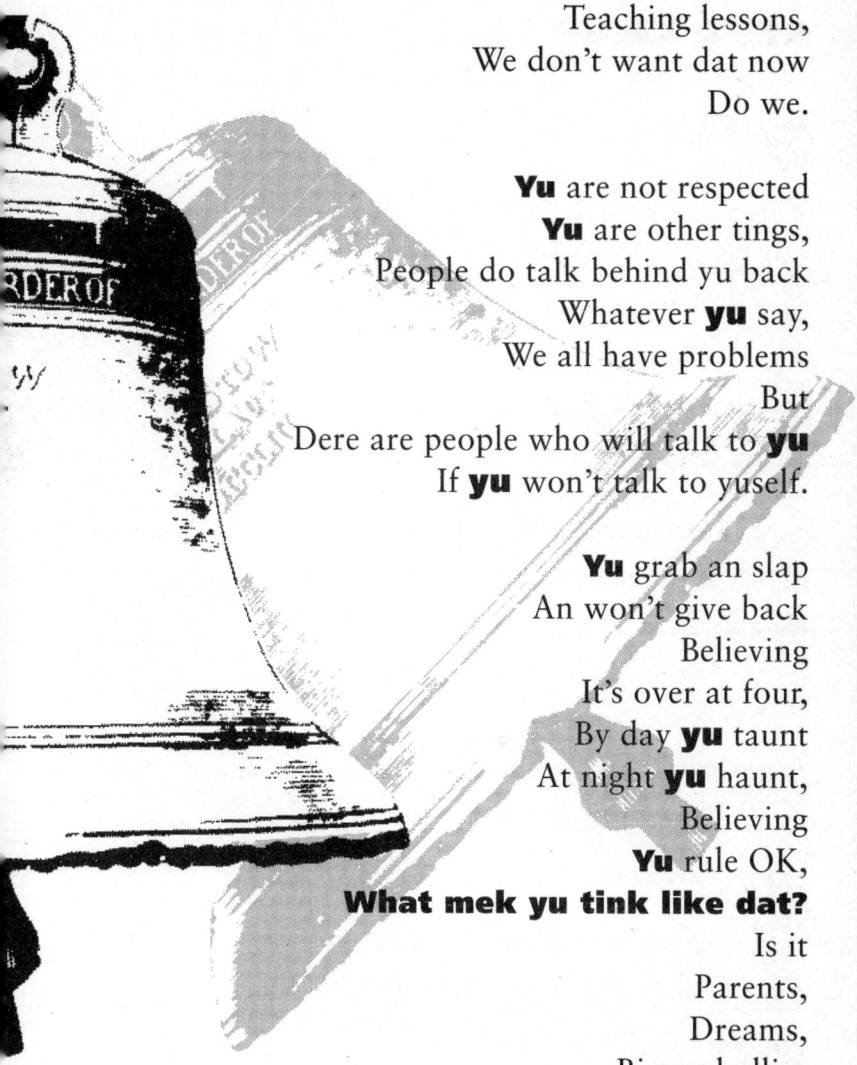

Teaching lessons,
We don't want dat now
Do we.

Yu are not respected
Yu are other tings,
People do talk behind yu back
Whatever **yu** say,
We all have problems
But
Dere are people who will talk to **yu**
If **yu** won't talk to yuself.

Yu grab an slap
An won't give back
Believing
It's over at four,
By day **yu** taunt
At night **yu** haunt,
Believing
Yu rule OK,
What mek yu tink like dat?
Is it
Parents,
Dreams,
Bigger bullies
Or television,
Who do we blame,
An
What mek yu tink like dat?

CIVIL LIES

Dear Teacher,

When I was born in Ethiopia
Life began,
As I sailed down the Nile civilization began,
When I stopped to think universities were built,
When I set sail
Asians and true Americans sailed with me.

When we traded nations were built,
We did not have animals,
Animals lived with us,
We had so much time
Thirteen months made our year,
We created social services
And cities that still stand.

So teacher do not say
Colombus discovered me
Check the great things I was doing
Before I suffered slavery.

Yours truly,

Mr Africa

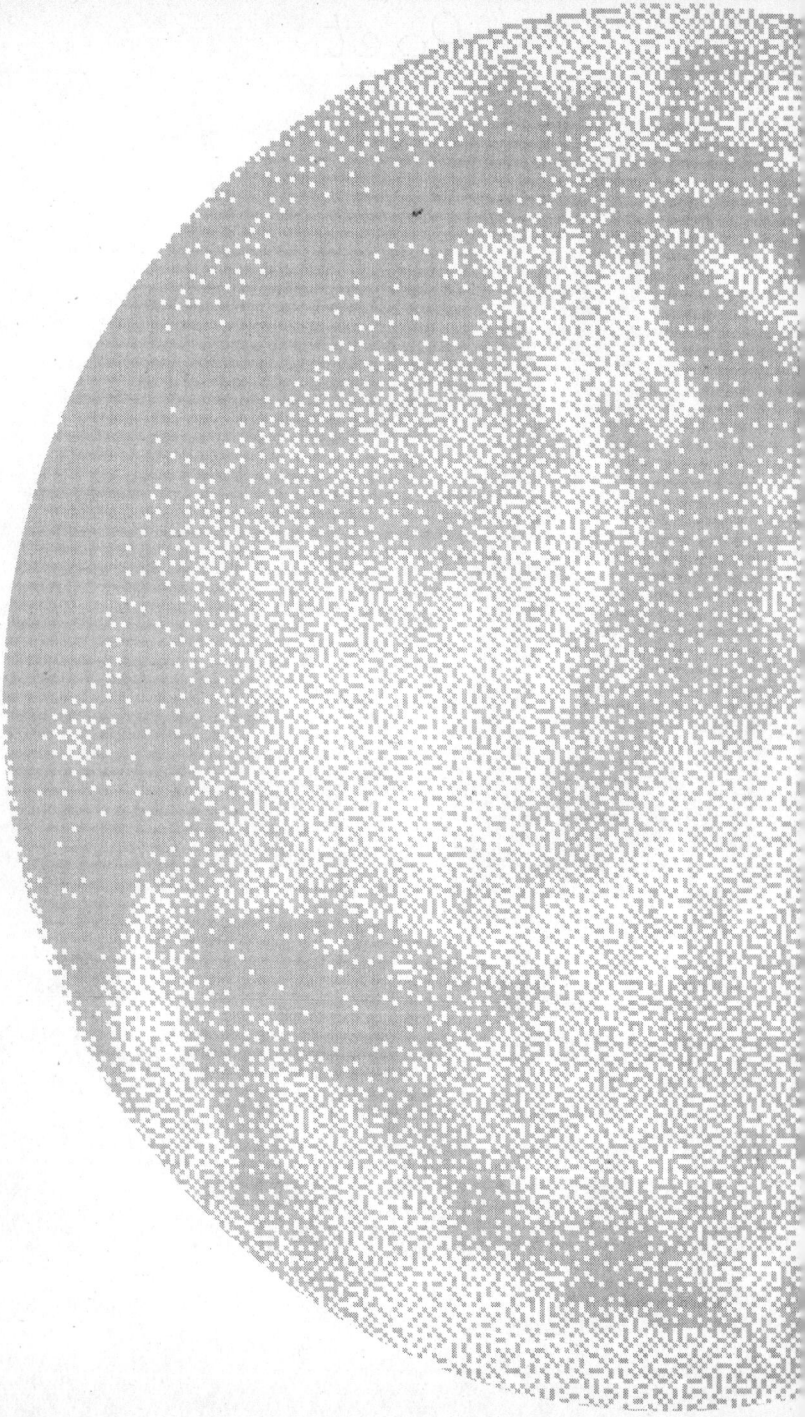

POEMS FROM THE LAST PERSON ON EARTH

FOR SALE

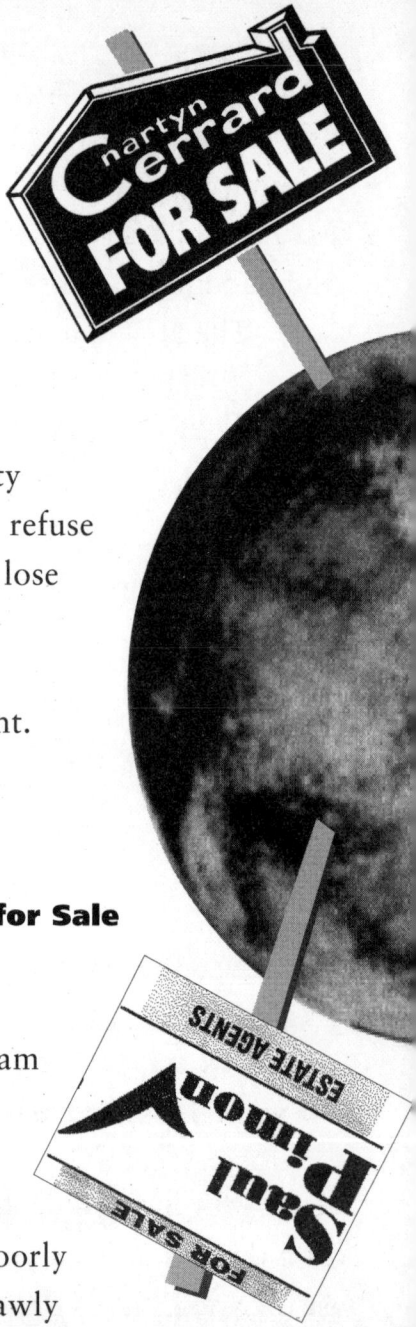

Looking for a bargain
Come on down
It's the Sale of the Century
Look around
There are sights to see
And places to be
With way out cosmic activity
This is a deal that you can't refuse
The kind of bet you cannot lose
So come on down
The price is right
I got to sell this thing tonight.

Chorus

Roll up, Roll up, Planet for Sale
Roll up, Planet for Sale.

Free of living things that roam
Free of people and ozone
I invite you to test my ware
Free of any atmosphere
Enjoy yourself as you get poorly
With no sign of a creepy crawly
I promise you will find no trees

And no flowers to make you sneeze.
Little Bo Peep has gone with her sheep
And little Jack Horner dissolved in a corner,
That Donald Duck has run out of luck
And Paddington Bear is no longer here
The Owl and the Pussy Cat went to sea
Then got lost in infinity.
Alive Alive no, Alive Alive no
Cockles and Mussels are not,
And no snow.

Chorus

Roll up, Roll up, Planet for Sale
Roll up, Planet for Sale.

Looking for a bargain, check this planet
Not a thing is moving on it
Just for you I'll do a deal
I'll swap it for a decent meal.

A BEETLE CALLED DEREK

There once was a Beetle called Derek
Who lived in a forest on Earth
And this little Beetle called Derek
Was really attracted to dirt,
She did not carry no weapons
Except what she naturally got
She did not have no possessions
But she could look after her lot.

The forest protected our Derek
Predators came and they went,
This was no reason to panic
Cause this was with Nature's consent,
She was related to Wind and Fire
A sister of necessity,
She was related to Earth and Water
A distant cousin to me.
Doctors could not work out Derek
Derek had secrets she kept,
Then came the white coated bandits
Scientists seeking all they could get,
Her home was robbed to make paper
And that got the climate upset,
Cows would graze to make burgers
The cows never made a profit!!

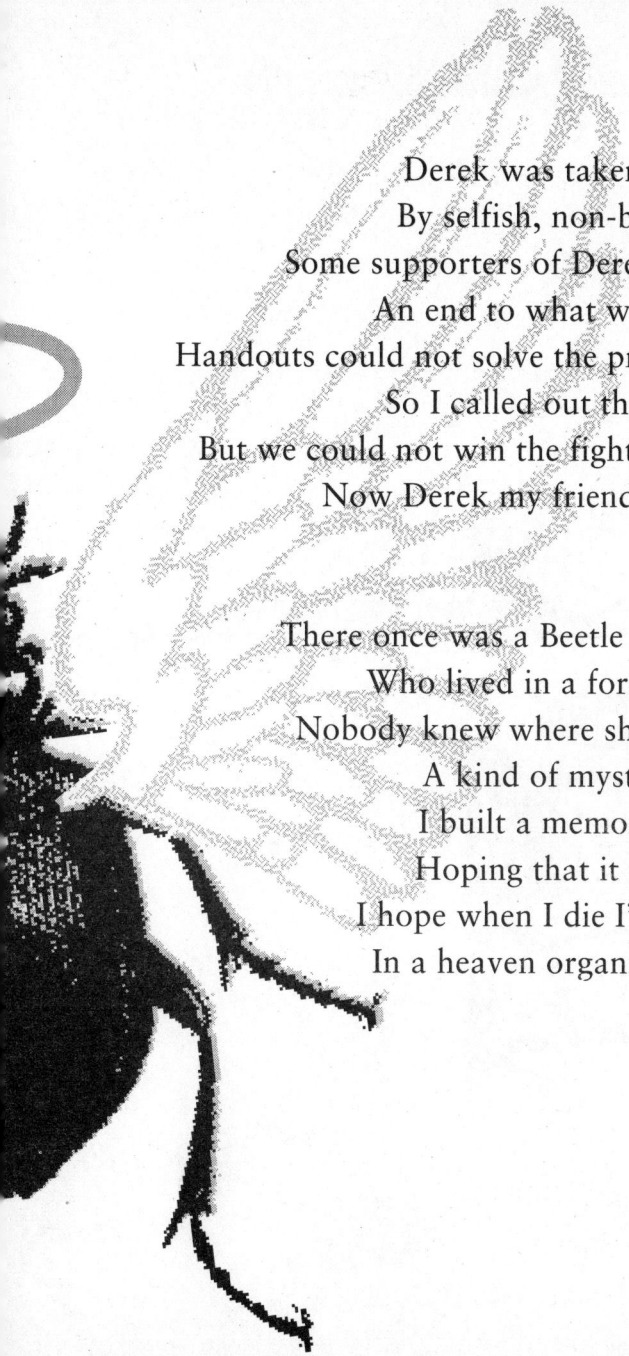

Derek was taken for granted
By selfish, non-beetle people,
Some supporters of Derek demanded
An end to what we called Evil,
Handouts could not solve the problem alone
So I called out the Eco-Police,
But we could not win the fight on our own
Now Derek my friend is deceased.

There once was a Beetle called Derek
Who lived in a forest on Earth,
Nobody knew where she came from
A kind of mysterious birth,
I built a memorial to Derek
Hoping that it may be seen,
I hope when I die I'll see Derek,
In a heaven organic and green.

BEAT IT

I broke my world record
I am famous for it
But now I am so bored
Cos I have no music.

PETS CONTROL

We moved into a house
We kicked de animals out,
Den we got our pets
An signed on at de vets,
We den called wild life strays
Zoos captured dem,
We gazed,
Wild life made great TV,
How civilized were we?

MEMORIES

I recall a time
Not long ago
When sheep would roam
around here,
If you were nice and friendly
You could get close to a deer,
Foxes, rabbits
Wild and free
We had so much potential,
But we did not live in harmony
And that was detrimental.
I take no blame
I did not do it
I was an innocent child,
My roots are very vegan
I like my animals wild,
I take no blame
I did not do it
I wrote to all the rulers,
I took a stand,
I loved the land
How I loved the Animal Kingdom.

I saw people training dogs
To make the doggies violent
Rulers of the land made dog
owners
Buy a licence,
I saw furs of animals
Upon human backs
I saw furs of animals
Being used as mats,
It happened here, I saw it
I called it Human Madness
I saw friends disappear
Imagine all my sadness,
I shouted from all high places
Let us not do this crime,
Nobody listened to me
Nobody had the time.

Memories don't leave like people do
I miss the kangaroo,
I recall great big trees,
I need these memories.

THINK ME

I want to be

In someone's mind

For ever

And ever

All right,

I want my picture taken

I must be someone's thought,

Somebody somewhere

Dream of me

I want to be

Remembered.

MORE TURKEY TALK

I

If
Big
Boys
Don't
Cry
.
.
Why
Do
I
?
.

LETTERS

I keep reading luv letters
So I won't feel alone,
I'll publish it an frame it
If I get one of me own.

KISS AN TELL

I kissed a girl
She nicked me tongue
It swept me off me feet,
It blew de air from out me lungs
An me heart missed a beat
Me liver quivered
Me legs shivered
Me head started swelling
Me eyes rolled back
Me back went crack
Den she started yelling,

'Clean your teeth!'

OVER DE MOON

Dere's a man on de moon
He's skipping an stuff,
Dere's a man on de moon
He looks very tuff,
Dere's a man on de moon
An he's all alone,
Dere's a man on de moon
His wife is at home.

He's dancing around
To real moony music,
He carries his air
He knows how to use it,
He waves to his wife
Still on Planet E,
She's waving back
But he cannot see.

De man on de moon is so clever,
He has sum ideas to persue,
His chewing gum can last fe ever
His fast food is already chewed.

Dere's a man on de moon
He has a spaceship,
Dere's a man on de moon
An we payed fe it,
Dere's a man on de moon
His mission ain't done,
Dere's a man on de moon
He's after de Sun.

MOVIE MADNESS

Jellybean one waz a blockbuster
Jellybean two waz a flop
Jellybean three a disaster
Jellybean four cost a lot
Jellybean five waz a miss take
Jellybean six was withdrawn
Jellybean seven a headache
Jellybean eight made us yawn.
Jellybean nine was just too much
Jellybean ten came and went
Jellybean films made me bankrupt
Because my film money's all spent.

Cinemas
ND BONUS OFFER
F PRICE all day Monday
£3.50 Tues-Fri
EFORE 6PM
Mon -Fri)
PANTON
ADVANCE BOOKING
081 970 6011
ADVANCE BOOKING
081 970 6032
NUS & ULU STUDENT DISCOUNT
JELLYBEAN
6
In Dolby Stereo
JELLYBEAN
SEVEN
JELLYBEAN
TOTTENHAM CT. RD.
CHEL
ADVANCE BOOKING
SEATS ONLY
JELLYBE
A TRUE STO
William Shakespe
JELLYBE
EIGHT
From Friday
From the creato
JELLYB
NI
1
PICCADILL
JELLYBE

FAIR PLAY

Mirror mirror on the wall
Could you please return our ball
Our football went through your crack
You have two now
Give one back.

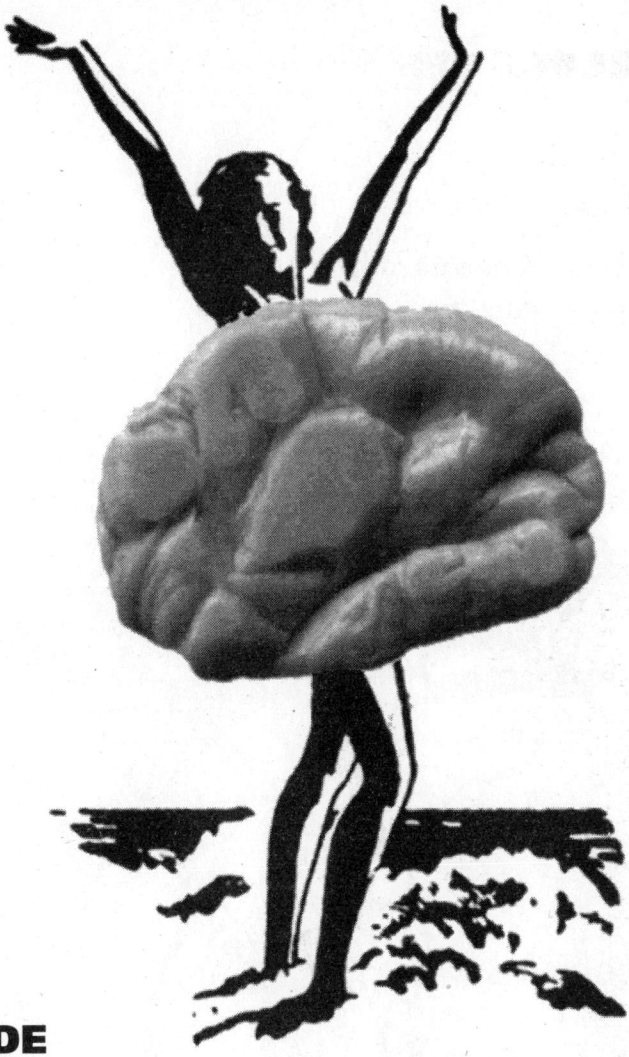

JUDE

Dere waz a cool dude called Jude
Who waz terribly awfully rude,
She spread bubble gum
All over her bum
An now she is stuck in de nude.

TELLING OFF

☞ Get your feet from **off** that table
Get your hands **out** of that pie
Get your teeth **out** of that apple
Get your things and say **goodbye**.

LUV SONG

I am in luv wid a hedgehog
I've never felt dis way before
I have luv fe dis hedgehog
An everyday I luv her more an more,
She lives by de shed
Where weeds an roses bed
An I just want de world to know
She makes me glow.

I am in luv wid a hedgehog
She's making me hair stand on edge,
So in luv wid dis hedgehog
An her friends
Who all live in de hedge
She visits me late
An eats off Danny's plate
But Danny's a cool tabby cat
He leaves it at dat.

I am in luv wid a hedgehog,
She's gone away so I must wait
But I do miss my hedgehog
Everytime she goes to hibernate.

EYE SEE

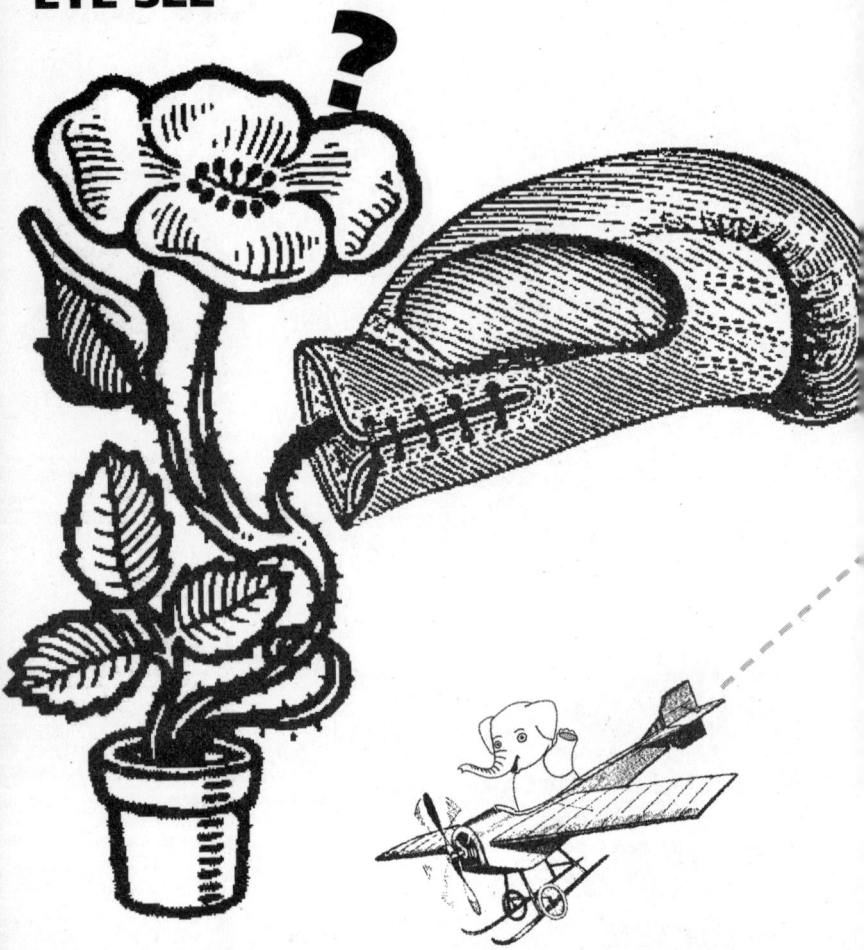

I've never seen flowers fight

It seems

Not all living things do,

I've never seen poodles get dressed

I have seen

Many well dressed,

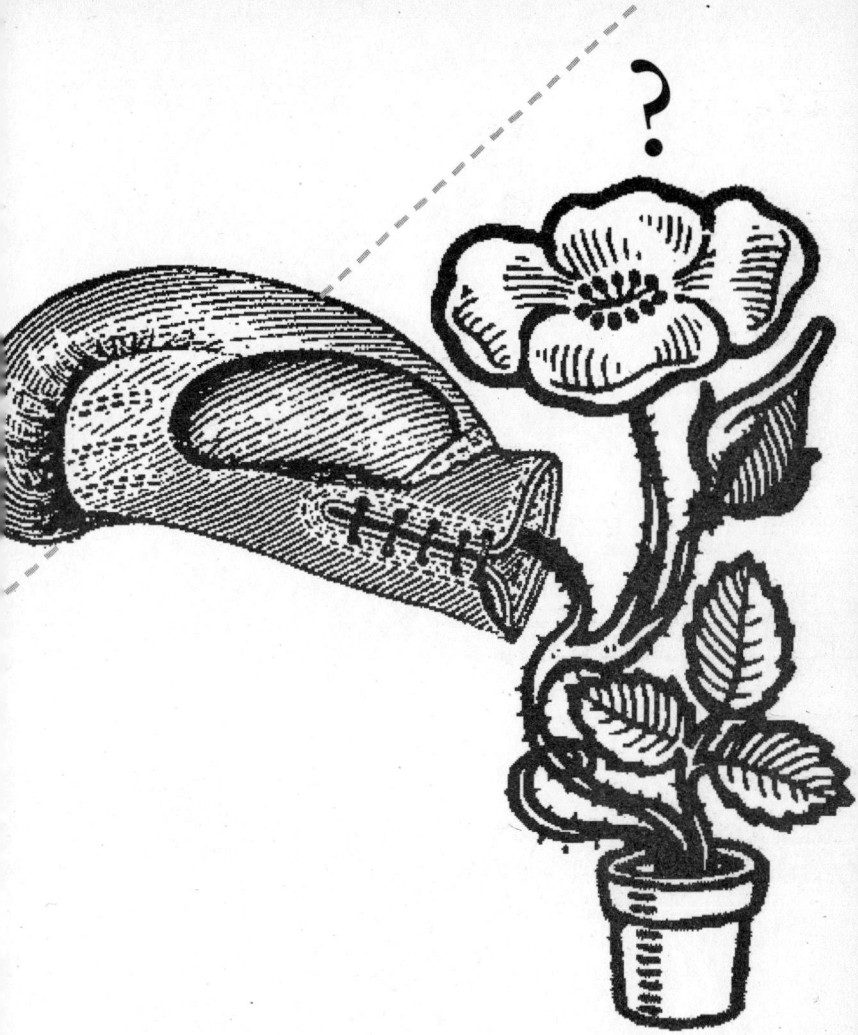

I have seen elephants fly

It seems

Not all people see what I see,

I've never seen a blind person lost

It seems

Only the sighted lose their way.

REMEMBRANCE DAYS

Ramadan in Pakistan
Is a special time
On Christmas Day in
Jamaica
The sun will always shine,
Diwali in India
Brings all the colours out
And don't forget
In Tibet
Each day
A Poet
Shouts.

Happy Birthday.

Today

You

Are

One

Day

Older,

Let's celebrate.

TALKING TURKEYS!!

Be nice to yu turkeys dis christmas
Cos turkeys jus wanna hav fun
Turkeys are cool, turkeys are wicked
An every turkey has a Mum.
Be nice to yu turkeys dis christmas,
Don't eat it, keep it alive,
It could be yu mate an not on yu plate
Say, Yo! Turkey I'm on your side.

I got lots of friends who are turkeys
An all of dem fear christmas time,
Dey wanna enjoy it, dey say humans destroyed it
An humans are out of dere mind,
Yeah, I got lots of friends who are turkeys
Dey all hav a right to a life,
Not to be caged up an genetically made up
By any farmer an his wife.

Turkeys jus wanna play reggae
Turkeys jus wanna hip-hop
Can yu imagine a nice young turkey saying,
'I cannot wait for de chop'?
Turkeys like getting presents, dey wanna
watch christmas TV,
Turkeys hav brains an turkeys feel pain
In many ways like yu an me.

I once knew a turkey called
Turkey
He said 'Benji explain to me please,
Who put de turkey in christmas
An what happens to christmas trees?'
I said, 'I am not too sure turkey
But it's nothing to do wid Christ Mass
Humans get greedy an waste more dan need be
An business men mek loadsa cash.'

Be nice to yu turkey dis christmas
Invite dem indoors fe sum greens
Let dem eat cake an let dem partake
In a plate of organic grown beans,
Be nice to yu turkey dis christmas
An spare dem de cut of de knife,
Join Turkeys United an dey'll be delighted
An yu will mek new friends '**FOR LIFE**'.

CHRISTMAS WISE

☆ All I **want** fe christmas is world peace
I **don't want** loads a food dat I really can't eat
All I **want** fe christmas is a long holiday
An a house in Jamaica where I can stay.
I **don't want** kisses under mistletoe from
Sloppy people I don't know,
I **won't** be putting out nu stocking cos
I **don't** wear de tings,
I **won't** be cutting down nu christmas trees,
I like dem living.

☆ All I **want** fe christmas is dis planet for ever
Fully complete wid its ozone layer
All I **want** fe christmas is friends and...
No more records from Status Quo,
I **don't want** a white christmas an I bet
We'll get nu more of dem cos of de Greenhouse effect,
An I **reckon** at christmas we create too much waste
Maybe a green christmas is more to my taste.
All I **want** fe christmas is sum honesty
About de wisdom of christmas
An how it should be
All I **want** fe christmas is clean air,
But I reckon I won't get none
An I don't think dat's fair.

SUNNYSIDE UP

When people
See people
Reading up
Side Down,
They think,
Maybe,
The reader
Can't read,
But
you should
Smile now,
Because you
Have found
A poem
That's out
To mislead.

ONCE UPON A TIME

I dreamt of living in a great big house
With a great big cat and a great big mouse
With a great big cupboard
Full of great big pears
I would grow great big
Without any cares.
Me great big hair on me great big head
Would feel great tucked into
Me great big bed
In me great bedroom
I would have great fights
With me big shadow
Who is really bright,
A great big sun shine would wake me up
I would drink great juice from a great big cup
And a great breakfast would make me feel great
And me school teachers would be always late.

I would speak great poems
With me great big voice
Great big hugs and kisses
Would make me feel nice
This great world would work together
as a team
I would live for ever
In me great big dream.

INDEX OF FIRST LINES

Ackees, chapatties 30
All I want fe christmas is world peace 90
An army of militant greens 46
Assalaam Alaikum 12
Be nice to yu turkeys dis christmas 88
Candyman, Candyman 34
Danny wakes up 36
Dat guy BAD 44
Dear Teacher 58
Dere waz a cool dude called Jude 81
Dere's a man on de moon 76
Dere's a Sonnet 14
Fed up with your old dog food 33
Funky monkey in the tree 22
Get your feet from off that table 82
Happy Birthday 87
He's a Fox Hunter, he said 52
Here we go 47
Heroes are funny people, dey are lost an found 54
I am in luv wid a hedgehog 83
I broke my world record 66
I dreamt of living in a great big house 93
I have poetic licence, i write the way i want 24
I keep reading luv letters 74
I kissed a girl 75
I really love chapatties 32
I recall a time 68

I reckon I could run de world **16**
I used to think nurses **48**
I want to be **70**
I went to Buckingham Palace today **26**
I wonder how babies are made **42**
I've never seen flowers fight **84**
If **74**
Jellybean one waz a blockbuster **78**
Life has its ups an downs **42**
Looking for a bargain **62**
Mirror mirror on the wall **80**
No Sir **28**
Ramadam in Pakistan **86**
Sociologists **43**
That's my little sister **20**
The dinosaurs are back **40**
The kids on our block are ok **32**
There once was a beetle called Derek **64**
Wanna be in our gang? **18**
We moved into a house **67**
We were born to rap **50**
When people **92**
Yu push **56**

READ MORE IN PUFFIN

For children of all ages, Puffin represents quality and variety – the very best in publishing today around the world.

For complete information about books available from Puffin – and Penguin – and how to order them, contact us at the appropriate address below. Please note that for copyright reasons the selection of books varies from country to country.

On the worldwide web: www.puffin.co.uk

In the United Kingdom: Please write to *Dept. EP, Penguin Books Ltd, Bath Road, Harmondsworth, West Drayton, Middlesex UB7 ODA*

In the United States: Please write to *Consumer Sales, Penguin USA, P.O. Box 999, Dept. 17109, Bergenfield, New Jersey 07621-0120.* VISA and MasterCard holders call 1-800-253-6476 to order Penguin titles

In Canada: Please write to *Penguin Books Canada Ltd, 10 Alcorn Avenue, Suite 300, Toronto, Ontario M4V 3B2*

In Australia: Please write to *Penguin Books Australia Ltd, P.O. Box 257, Ringwood, Victoria 3134*

In New Zealand: Please write to *Penguin Books (NZ) Ltd, Private Bag 102902, North Shore Mail Centre, Auckland 10*

In India: Please write to *Penguin Books India Pvt Ltd, 706 Eros Apartments, 56 Nehru Place, New Delhi 110 019*

In the Netherlands: Please write to *Penguin Books Netherlands bv, Postbus 3507, NL-1001 AH Amsterdam*

In Germany: Please write to *Penguin Books Deutschland GmbH, Metzlerstrasse 26, 60594 Frankfurt am Main*

In Spain: Please write to *Penguin Books S. A., Bravo Murillo 19, 1° B, 28015 Madrid*

In Italy: Please write to *Penguin Italia s.r.l., Via Felice Casati 20, I–20124 Milano.*

In France: Please write to *Penguin France S. A., 17 rue Lejeune, F–31000 Toulouse*

In Japan: Please write to *Penguin Books Japan, Ishikiribashi Building, 2–5–4, Suido, Bunkyo-ku, Tokyo 112*

In South Africa: Please write to *Longman Penguin Southern Africa (Pty) Ltd, Private Bag X08, Bertsham 2013*